AMAZING|WAVES

THE BEAUTY OF WAVES AND AN APPRECIATION OF SURF

BY ROGER SHARP

AMAZING WAVES

ISBN: 978-0-9930383-1-0
PUBLISHED BY:
Orca Publications
Berry Road Studios
Berry Road
Newquay
TR7 1AT
United Kingdom

TEL: +44 (0)1637 878074
www.orcasurf.co.uk

EDITOR: Roger Sharp
DESIGNER: David Alcock

CONTRIBUTING PHOTOGRAPHERS: Helio Antonio, Bastien Bonnarme, Chris Burkard, Andrew
Chisholm, Damian Davila, Alan van Gysen, Timo Jarvinen, Mike Lacey, Rodd Owen, Marcus Paladino,
Laurent Pujol, Roger Sharp, Andrew Shield, Trent Slatter, Josh Tabone, Ben Thouard

PRINTED BY: Great Wall Printing, Hong Kong

COVER ARGUABLY THE MOST BEAUTIFUL AND DEADLY WAVE IN THE WORLD:
TEAHUPO'O OFF THE SOUTH COAST OF THE MAIN ISLAND OF TAHITI. PHOTO: BEN THOUARD
OPPOSITE COOK ISLANDS. PHOTO: JOSH TABONE
FOLLOWING SPREAD TAHITI. PHOTO: BEN THOUARD

AMAZING|WAVES

THE BEAUTY OF WAVES AND AN APPRECIATION OF SURF

FOREWORD_

THE NATURAL WORLD IS FULL OF WONDERS. THE AWESOME POWER AND SUBLIME BEAUTY OF WAVES IS ONE OF THE MOST ENTHRALLING PLANETARY PROCESSES.

Whether you're a surfer or have never even seen the sea, you can't help but be transfixed by the aquatic sculptures of infinite variety that are waves. Their spellbinding, shimmering dance makes writers reach for the thesaurus and artists for their palettes. Photographers dedicate their lives to capturing their majesty. Wherever there's enough fetch to blow swell into existence you can find waves. It's these salty shape-shifters and the people that document them that this book is dedicated to. If you enjoy the book please take the time to follow the talented crew of photographers whose work graces these pages. They're aquatic artists of note and their images will make your mind glow.

INTRODUCTION_

For many of us, our earliest memories of the beach are of jumping over waves. Even as infants we notice the peculiar rhythm of the ocean and how the waves come in groups. The green flag days when we were allowed to play were relished. Red flag days when the waves were too dangerous were marvelled at.

This fascination with ocean energy leads people to become wave-riders, swimmers, lifeguards and even surf photographers. Seeking out waves of all shapes and sizes is what we do. Our connection to the ocean is strong. Knowing how waves work is essential, playing in their power is one of the most exciting things you can do, however you choose to do it. This book is a celebration of the raw beauty of waves around the world, so dive in and get salty.

INDONESIA. PHOTO: TIMO JARVINEN

AUSTRALIA. PHOTO: JOSH TABONE

THURSO, SCOTLAND. PHOTO: ROGER SHARP

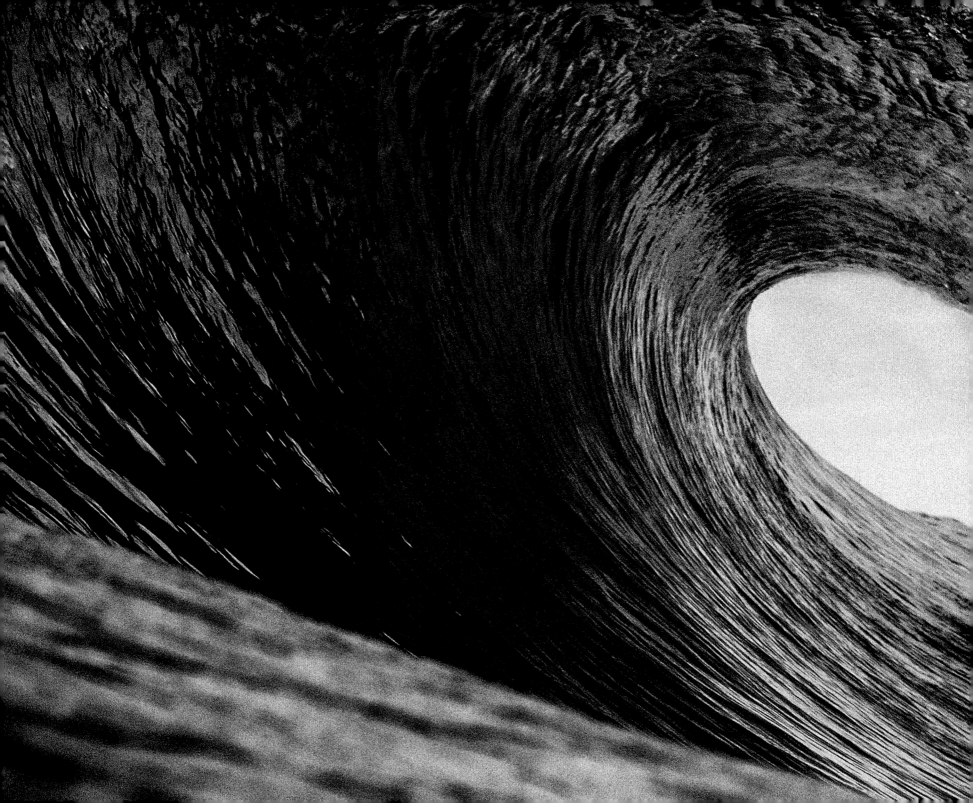

PREVIOUS SPREAD GUMS, HAWAII. PHOTO: TIMO JARVINEN
RIGHT PIPELINE, HAWAII. PHOTO: JOSH TABONE
FOLLOWING SPREAD JEFFREY'S BAY, SOUTH AFRICA. PHOTO: ALAN VAN GYSEN

14

TEAHUPO'O, TAHITI. PHOTO: BEN THOUARD

BASS STRAIT, AUSTRALIA. PHOTO: ANDREW SHIELD

TEAHUPO'O, TAHITI. PHOTO BEN THOUARD

SEARCHING
FOR WAVES_

Waves can be found anywhere there's a body of water

The search for waves has been ongoing since the surf culture gripped the world fifty years ago. Surfers spend their lives obsessed with seeking new waves and scoring their favourite spots on the best days. Surf photographers have joined in the search, but with the added caveat of planning the best light and weather as well. All-in-all capturing the best waves is a tricky thing. Especially as some waves only break once every few years. Even the big name spots can have bad seasons or just have poor conditions for months on end – especially when strong El Niño or La Niña events are interfering with the global weather patterns.

Scoring waves is all about being on top of your knowledge. Where to be and when to be is key. So it follows that wave hounds are weather geeks of the highest order. Any spot has a favoured swell direction, size and a complementary wind direction.

Learning these for your home spots takes time. Expand your horizons around the world and you really need an almanac to keep your notes in. For shooting photos the position of the sun is also vital. The early morning or evening light 'golden hour' tends to deliver the best colour.

Finding waves used to be word of mouth; then came the surf magazines and films, and now with Google Earth and social media, finding good spots is a doddle. That said, it still takes going out a on a limb and exploring to find the real gold. Plenty of incredible spots haven't got their own car park, surf forecast page on the Internet or an entry in a guidebook. Obviously it's your responsibility not to blow the cover of the off-the-radar spots. Particularly if you're taking photos, avoid giveaway landmarks in your images. Tread lightly with social media also, especially when it comes to having the GPS and location services turned on in your phone or camera. Leave the adventure of finding waves for those that come after you.

Of course, some photogenic waves aren't even remotely surfable, so you have to find those locales for yourself. Part of the joy of being a wave watcher, surfer or photographer (or all three at the same time) is getting to immerse yourself in, and explore, our coastlines' more untouched aspects.

Countless film frames and millions of megabytes of data documenting waves have been racked up in Hawaii, Tahiti, California, Australia, South Africa and all over Europe. Now the search continues into deeper, harder to get to spots, and with the more precise nature of forecasting, missions to waves that rarely break can be plotted with more confidence. Have all the great waves in the world been found? Probably not. All the consistent ones? Quite possibly.

Incredible waves are out there; we're just like bird spotters hunting elusive species across continents. You have to use knowledge and experience to hopefully be in the right place at the right time for the exotic ones. While at home it's just about having fun in the brine when the conditions are at their best.

SCOTLAND. PHOTO: ROGER SHARP

HISTORIC WAVES_

Waves and us through the ages

As a species we've been fascinated with waves ever since our brain matter has been complex enough to observe the natural world. For thousands of years we've admired their beauty, played in their energy and respected their power.

Our continents and coastlines are sculpted by waves. Their relentless power is constantly reshaping our world. Grinding rock into sand to be made into rock again. Waves of all sizes are recycling the planet in geological time and defining the edges of our domain.

Throughout history we've sought shelter from waves, developing ports and harbours where they couldn't unleash their damage, so shipping could carry on safely. The development of trade in ancient cultures relates to how easily navigable the seas were. Parts of the world without much surf, such as the Mediterranean, were therefore the focus for the development of civilisation and trade. Now, as we move forward, harnessing the incredible force of waves to power our homes could become a vital part of our renewable era.

Enjoying waves is a relatively recent phenomenon for most, as is forecasting them, yet in some parts of the world using waves for fun stretches back millennia. No one is entirely sure where the wave sliding art of surfing was first practised. The archaeology boffins concur that the ancient Polynesians and Peruvians have the leading claims.

Surfing – or *he'e nalu*, in Hawaiian dialect – was first recorded in European culture in 1769, by Joseph Banks of the HMS Endeavour. It was during a stop in Tahiti, on one of Captain Cook's explorations, that he marvelled at the locals bodysurfing and using a broken piece of canoe to ride the waves: "In the midst of these breakers 10 or 12 Indians were swimming who, whenever a surf broke near them, dived under it with infinite ease, rising up on the other side; but their chief amusement was carried on by the stern of an old canoe; with this before them they swam out as far as the outermost breach, then one or two would get into it and opposing the blunt end to the breaking wave were hurried in with incredible swiftness."

Precisely how long the Polynesians practised the art is unknown, but it's thought to go back thousands of years. One theory is that fishermen used boards to get back into shore easily with their catch. Outrigger canoes hollowed out from logs can also surf waves to let the paddler save energy.

Similarly, in the Pre-Incan civilisation, the Mochica, then Chimu cultures fished from their *Caballitos de Totora* and surfed them back to shore. These vessels are basically like wave-skis constructed from reeds, and are still made today.

As the Polynesians spread throughout the Pacific they took their wave-riding skills with them, and gradually the pastime became shaped more like the wave sliding we know today in Hawaii. The 'sport of kings' was a large part of island culture and after a hiatus – thanks to suppression by western influence – was revived. It spread around the world in the 20th century thanks to Hawaiian ambassadors like George Freeth and Duke Kahanamoku.

During the last century a revered ancient pastime turned brief tourist novelty from Waikiki, has spread around the globe and wave riding now exists on pretty much every coast where waves break.

HAWAIIAN SURFING SKETCH EARLY 19TH CENTURY.
ILLUSTRATION: BERNICE PAUAHI BISHOP MUSEUM

AUSTRALIA. PHOTO: JOSH TABONE

AUSTRALIA. PHOTO: RODD OWEN

EDDYSTONE ROCK, TASMANIA. PHOTO: ANDREW CHISHOLM

LEFT NEW SOUTH WALES, AUSTRALIA. PHOTO: JOSH TABONE
RIGHT DUNES, SOUTH AFRICA. PHOTO: ALAN VAN GYSEN
FOLLOWING SPREAD DONKEY BAY, NAMIBIA. PHOTO: ALAN VAN GYSEN

ABOVE **PORTHTOWAN, CORNWALL.** PHOTO: ROGER SHARP

RIGHT **AUSTRALIA.** PHOTO: RODD OWEN

FOLLOWING SPREAD **OCCY'S LEFT, INDONESIA.** PHOTO: RODD OWEN

TAHITI. PHOTO: BEN THOUARD

HOW TO
SHOOT WAVES_

Tips and tricks for shooting swell pictures

The world of photography has survived the bumpy transition from film to digital and images are now easier to create than ever before. Especially as the majority of us have a decent quality camera in our pockets at all times. While retro kids are experimenting with film again, the old photography adage, 'the best camera is the one you have with you', makes a lot of sense. You don't need a two-grand, state-of-the-art DSLR camera to take amazing wave images. A humble GoPro can produce magic, as can a £50 manual film camera from a charity shop in a homemade lunchbox housing. Here are some pointers on the various methods used by pros and amateurs alike in their search for the perfect wave photo.

LAND: **Long Lens**

Shooting waves is possible with pretty much any equipment. The surf photographer's standard long lens, anything from 300mm to 800mm, is handy for picking out tubular moments. Filling the frame and waiting for the killer wave are key tactics. It's the least exciting way of shooting, but on big days definitely the safest. A camera with a fast frame rate is your friend here, as picking out that key moment is tricky without a

surfer to reference. The 'looking into Waimea Shorebreak' is the all-time classic long lens wave image.

LAND: **Line-Ups**

One of the modern masters of the line-up is Chris Burkard. He's made the environmental line-up slash action shot one of the most emulated in the game. He wasn't the first to forage in the Arctic fringes, but his cold wanderings and line-ups featuring snow-capped mountains with frosty barrels reeling off in the foreground helped nudge surf magazines' image selection up a gear.

A line-up shot should be National Geographic worthy; a flawless wave, well timed with the light and clouds; a shot that makes the viewer want to dive through the page, or screen, and fall over themselves in the rush to paddle out.

The mid-range lenses, 35 to 135mm, are your go-to for these shots. A good line-up is a thing of beauty and the key is composition. Getting some foreground interest to frame your dream line-up adds to the story of an image, and a surfer is always handy for scale. Study the shots in this book for pointers.

ALAN VAN GYSEN

WATER: **Fisheye**

The fisheye rig is a default in surf photography, like the long lens set up for land shots. The 180-degree field of view from corner to corner, teamed with a deep depth of field, means photographers can be mere inches away from a surfer and still get a sharp image. For wave shots fisheyes are brilliant at capturing empty caverns and making the most of closeouts. Composure is learnt the hard way, as you don't look through the camera. But the beauty of a fisheye is that if you're pointing it vaguely in the right direction, something good should happen. Top tip: if you're right-handed shooting a right-handed wave, so the wave is coming towards you, tilt the housing 20 to 30 degrees out to sea. Then as the wave picks you up and you shoot, the horizon won't be wonky.

Also, lick the port. Keep it licked. No more beads of water. Don't muck about with potatoes or toothpaste. This is known as running a wet port.

ROGER SHARP

WATER: **Medium Lens**

Wide angle to standard optics, between 20mm and 50mm, are all useful tools for capturing the wonder of waves. You can use them as a replacement for a fisheye on bigger

LAURENT PUJOL

days, when getting super deep is tricky, or on beaches where holding position is hard. They're also great for shallow depth-of-focus shots on smaller days. Thankfully they're good bang for your buck and also really compact and light, which makes them easy for swimming. For any lens that's not a fisheye you use a flat port, as opposed to a dome, and it's best to run them dry, as opposed to wet as you would with a dome. Every photographer will have their own secret tip for this, but rubbing finger grease in then buffing it off pre-swim works a treat. Water beads off and you don't get any blobs.

WATER: **Long Lens**

Longer lenses in the water are really useful for picking out detail and texture in waves. A 70-200mm with a zoom control on the housing gives you a lot of options for shooting in a range of conditions. From tight work on smaller days to shooting bigger days from the safety of the channel, it's a good set up to have in your arsenal. You'll also develop some good guns, as the rig weighs a ton. Relatively light options are the 85mm/f1.8 and 100mm/f2 fast lenses, which give great image quality but don't break the bank.

WATER: **Pujol Style**

The newest and hardest style of surf photography is only being pursued by a handful of shooters. It's dangerous, unpredictable and scary, and involves guaranteed beatings. But that's why the shots by Laurent Pujol and, latterly, young Australian kid Leroy Bellet, are shoe-ins for magazine covers around the world. The technique requires advanced surfing skill and lots of mates, as you need to tow-in behind the surfer and shoot them before the inevitable drubbing. Not so much use for empty wave shots unless you're a real masochist with access to a jet ski.

JOSH TABONE

WATER: **Underwater**

A decent mask is key to shooting waves from under the surface. The Aquasphere goggles that don't cover your nose like the more bulky scuba masks do are ideal. Once you can see in the underwater realm it's just a case of getting inventive. The focus is the hard part to nail due to the different refractive indices of water. Try focusing your lens at 30cm and see how you

go. That's generally a good ballpark for sharp underwater images. When you've done it once you'll be addicted. All you need is crystal clear water like Tahiti, or the far reaches of the Scottish islands.

WATER: **GoPro**

The GoPro has developed from a comical wrist-mounted stills camera to the moneymaker for a state-of-the-art billion-dollar company. These little units are incredibly rich in tech for the price. Anything from the Hero 4 Black upwards gives awesome quality stills and video. For the price they

can't be beaten. And the work being produced by folks all over the world on Instagram is testament to how good they are. The key thing is diving into the settings and giving yourself the most control possible. That and a decent accessory rig for shooting.

WATER: **iPhone**

The camera on the current iPhone is pretty damn amazing. Chuck it in

BEN THOUARD

a waterproof case like those made by Aquatech and you can use it to shoot waves. Zak Noyle has even shot Pipeline with his. The current model is technically waterproof but not enough for getting lipped by waves. So best not to try without a case fit for purpose.

WATER: **Jetski**

Shooting from a ski is all good, as long as the ski is behaving. They're unreliable beasts and there's nowt worse than being on one that's decided to give up the ghost with expensive camera gear. Depending on the spot, you can either shoot with a housing or whack your naked camera in a Pelican case. Driving yourself is preferable to being driven, as sitting pillion is tricky. A ski is great way of being in the thick of it on big days, but if you're on a ski then by default you're part of the safety team. So training on pick ups, CPR and first aid are essential. Top tip: get a dive belt and karabiner swim fins on it –

very handy for the inevitable break down and the long swim back to the harbour towing the ski.

WATER: **Boat**

Shooting from a boat, like the chaps in the channel at Teahupo'o, is thrilling. It can also be very dangerous. It all depends on the skill of your boat driver and the reliability of the boat. You can gauge pretty quickly if a driver knows what he's doing. Shooting with a waterproof Pelican case is essential, so in the event of something going wrong your gear is safe and you've also got a handy life float if there are no lifejackets... and there rarely are on Indo tenders. Getting the angle is the hard part with boats, and that all comes down to communication with the driver. Beware of ramping over waves, as gravity can be a bitch. Also, try and park up if you can, as constant petrol engine fumes and noise ruin the tranquillity of a session.

AIR: **Drone**

The newest tool in the forward-thinking photographer's arsenal is the unmanned aerial vehicle. Initially unwieldy tools that needed a professional radio control background to work, they're now so simple that anyone can fly one with a few minutes' practice. They're not cheap and do not like salt water. Also, if you intend to sell images or get them published, you need to complete a course and get your license. So get permission for commercial operation from the Civil Aviation Authority.

Overall the image quality is getting really good and a whole new world of line-ups and aerial wave work is unfolding. Ensure your drone can shoot raw for the best quality and always follow local regulations.

AIR: **Helicopter**

Possibly the most fun way to shoot waves, but sadly difficult to justify now that drones offer aerial images without the massive hassle of organising a chopper. The obvious advantage is shooting with a proper DSLR and the quality that brings, as well as being able to choose lenses. For the full heli experience request that the doors are off, so you can shoot without hassle. This does mean you'll possibly soil yourself – as being in a helicopter with the door off is both incredible fun and terrifying.

Top tip: Don't have lens caps to deal with, as they'll blow away. Helicopters are the key to those incredible Californian line-ups of Ventura and Rincon stacked with lines to the horizon.

WESTERN AUSTRALIA. PHOTO: RYAN MILLER

"

TO ME A GOOD WAVE PHOTO IS STILL A
PICTURE OF A WAVE THAT IS SURFABLE.
OR AT LEAST LOOKS LIKE IT MIGHT
BE... YOU CAN ADD ANY COMBINATION
OF AMAZING LIGHT, WATER CLARITY
OR EXOTIC LOCATION BUT THE KEY
INGREDIENT IS THE MIND-SURF FACTOR.

"

- ANDREW SHIELD

PREVIOUS SPREAD EAST COAST, SOUTH AFRICA. PHOTO: ALAN VAN GYSEN
RIGHT KIRRA, AUSTRALIA. PHOTO: ANDREW SHIELD
FOLLOWING SPREAD ANCHOVIES, SOLOMON ISLANDS. PHOTO: ANDREW SHIELD

MAVERICKS, CALIFORNIA. PHOTO: BASTIEN BONNARME

FORECASTING
WAVES_

Why D-Day brought us swell forecasts

In the 21st century, if we want to know what the waves are doing anywhere on Earth we just need to go online. Literally anywhere in the world can be checked within a few minutes. You can find out the current conditions, buoy data, local winds and the forecast for the next week. All with reasonable accuracy, sometimes even with a live HD webcam.

It wasn't always so...

The British Met Office is the original weather forecasting operation. It was established in 1854 as part of the Board of Trade, to look into the possibility of forecasting the weather to serve mariners. Its focus on waves and storms sharpened in October 1859 with the loss of the Royal Charter – a ship that went down in a storm off Anglesey, Wales, tragically killing 459 souls. This was a tipping point and a gale warning system utilising 15 manned coastal stations was established, to alert ships to potential ruin. The established coastguard lookouts at the time were more concerned with smuggling and rescue rather than prevention.

The first public weather forecast was published in *The Times* on 1 August 1861, by Vice-Admiral Robert Fitzroy. He set up the Met Office and laid the foundations for the science of meteorology, and also captained Darwin's famous voyage of the HMS Beagle. His forecasts weren't renowned for accuracy, and sometimes derided, as the tools at his disposal were limited; but his vision set the course. Not much has changed in 150 years, as we still all love to scoff at a bad forecast.

As the science of meteorology, wireless telegraphy and shipping improved, the key to any forecast – data – became more bountiful. Ships could telegraph the wind speed/direction, barometric pressure and an overall idea of the weather systems ascertained. The first BBC Radio weather broadcast came in November 1922 and, with the exception of during World War II, has been broadcast every day since. The shipping forecast, part of the very fabric of British culture, started in October 1925. TV forecasts came along in 1949.

Swell forecasting, like a lot of technological advances, came from the military. It wasn't until World War II that forecasting waves as a science really started. The focus was on making sure conditions would be safe for landing craft during invasions. As you can imagine, a beach assault with a lot of swell would be treacherous.

The Met Office became a branch of the military late in the 19th century, and divided into air and naval arms in 1936, key as it was for any operation. With the tide of the war turning, British Navy Commander Claude Suthons was charged with the task of figuring out the wave prediction dilemma. He came up with basic charts to relate wave height and period to the duration and fetch of the wind.

US Army Air Force scientist Professor Harald Sverdrup and his apprentice, Walter Munk, came up with a similar process. But this was all based on observation and not totally accurate equations on the complex process of how waves generate and propagate. The network of 58 observation stations did give them enough data to get a handle on the swell in the English Channel, which was the vital part.

TAHITI. PHOTO: BEN THOUARD

Pressing the go button for the D-Day landings had to coincide with a small day of waves, and the team involved delivered arguably the most important weather forecast ever. A predicted, narrow window of calm led to Eisenhower calling the invasion at the last minute, changing the course of history.

Sverdrup, Munk and another colleague, Charles Bretschneider, continued their research after the war and are the pioneers upon whose work the discipline of modelling swell is built on. The field continued to be researched and refined over the next couple of decades, leading eventually to the WAM system (Wave Amplitude Model). With the advent of the Internet and computer power increasing finally, the complicated maths and data sets could be visualised. The US Navy's Fleet Numerical Meteorological and Oceanographic Centre (FNMOC) made their WAM data available to the public in 1994, and ever since then we've been more clued up than ever. Satellite data has been the cherry on top, with advances being made year on year. Initially satellite imagery helped forecasters figure out cloud cover and how active storms were, whereas newer satellites can now measure wave heights. So near real-time swell data worldwide is finally a reality.

Older surfers relied on forecasting using isobar pressure maps from weather faxes and yelling at Bill Giles to get out of the way of the Atlantic synoptic chart. The dark art of working out fetch and swell direction, matched with local knowledge of where might be good, is on the wane. The steady advance of technology has made swell forecasting less of a gamble and more of a certainty. All you need is a glance of your smartphone wherever you are in the world – as long as you've got mobile signal or Wi-Fi.

But even with all the science perfected, the supercomputers and Earth observing satellites in existence, the forecast sites still get it wrong quite frequently. Weather models are just that – a probability, a version that might come to pass. Sometimes you've just got to go to the beach and have a look. Which is kind of cool.

AUSTRALIA. PHOTO: RODD OWEN

THE BOOM, NICARAGUA. PHOTO: ROGER SHARP

TELOS, INDONESIA. PHOTO: ANDREW SHIELD

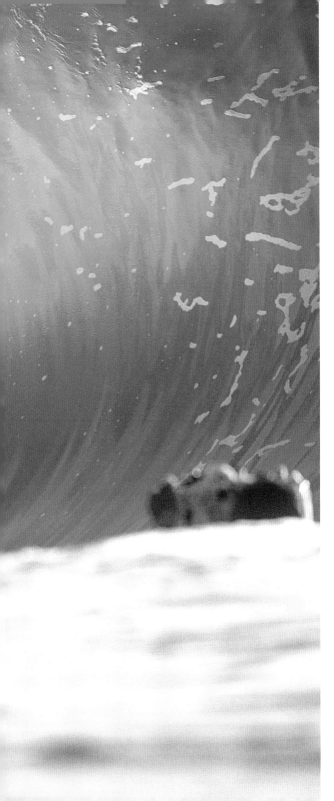

RILEYS, IRELAND. PHOTO: LAURENT PUJOL

"
PRETTY MUCH EVERYTHING HAS TO
DO WITH THE LIGHT; IF YOU CAN
GET EPIC LIGHT AND AN EPIC WAVE
YOU'RE WELL ON YOUR WAY TO GETTING
A MAD IMAGE. THE REST IS UP TO YOU
TO WORK THE ANGLES!
"
- ANDREW CHISHOLM

THE POINTS, AUSTRALIA. PHOTO: ANDREW CHISHOLM

TAHITI. PHOTO: BEN THOUARD

IRELAND. PHOTO: ROGER SHARP

WHY WAVES HAPPEN_

Here comes the science bit

Without any wind there would only be one oceanic wave on Earth and that's the tide. With a wavelength of 20,000km it's quite hard to spot. Thankfully, this is not the case.

Our planet is lucky that it has abundant water, which we can credit to volcanic activity and plate tectonics. It also sits in the sweet spot in the solar system where water is in a liquid state and, for the bulk of us, in between ice ages as we are, not too frozen. Which means it's free to create waves. We're also blessed with an atmosphere that can generate weather.

However, it's down to some other waves to initiate the whole process: light waves. The energy from the sun reaches us from near 150 million kilometres away in all of eight minutes and 20 seconds. Which is a fair clip. Being able to travel through a vacuum, unlike a lot of other waves,

helps. Light waves are transverse waves, just like the oceanic kind, and like ocean waves they can be reflected and refracted.

This electromagnetic radiation from the sun heats the Earth's surface, which in turn warms the air; and it's redistribution of this heat that gives us pressure systems. Colder air sinks in the polar regions, creating high pressure, and rises in the hotter equatorial regions to give us lows. Without it we'd have no wind or weather. A small-scale example is a sea breeze: as the land heats up the air rises, pulling in the colder air from over the sea. This process happens on a vast scale globally. It's the dance of pressure systems, assisted by the Coriolis effect deflecting wind flow predominantly west in the Northern Hemisphere, which gives us the wind to create waves.

To actually make a wave takes mass. Throw a rock in a pond and the mass displaces the water to make ripples. The mass of air acting on the ocean works in the same way. The lightest breeze can make tiny capillary waves; gently blow on your next cup of tea to see how little force it takes. Even the mightiest swell begins as a tiny wave somewhere – purely

from the friction between the air and the water.

The waves we are interested in are created in by the wind blowing over an area of ocean for an amount of time. There are the three factors that count: wind speed, fetch and duration.

Tiny capillary waves become chop, which in turn coalesce to become wind waves, and given enough energy can become ocean-crossing swell. Which is what wave junkies prefer. Without the requisite energy, wind waves will die down, thanks to surface tension, once they leave

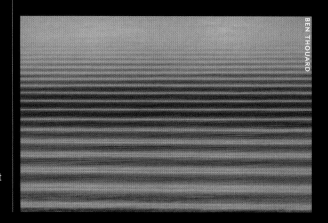

BEN THOUARD

the storm. Swells however, with the energy required, escape the storm that birthed them and can cross whole oceans. As an example, Southern Ocean storms off Antarctica can generate swells that can reach Alaska.

An in-depth look at the mind-bending science of swell formation is outside the remit of this book, but there are plenty of resources online and British big wave surfer/scientist, Dr Tony Butt, has written an excellent Surf Science book that explains all.

It's when swell hits the coast that we get waves. Waves can refract and reflect, and the local topography dictates how swell interacts with land in its final moments. Shallow continental shelves slow waves down, as in British waters. Whereas oceanic islands, like Hawaii, have no shelf and the waves' full energy arrives at the reefs to give spectacular displays like Pipeline. Famously the waves at Nazaré and Hossegor have more punch because offshore canyons refract the swells to make wedges.

Of course the shape of the shore makes a huge difference. The classic spilling, surging or pitching waves from school science are all due to the steepness of the beach or reef. The range of breaks is evidenced throughout this book: beaches, reefs, point breaks, slabs, river mouths, sandbars formed by longshore drift (even this is the act of tiny waves) and more. Although our attempts at sea defences tend to mess up the waves, sometimes it works in our favour, such as at the Wedge and Sandspit in California. Using dynamite to blow channels for boats in reefs has also created some more useful waves to surfers.

Local wind also influences the shape of waves. Offshore wind cleans up the waves and is the optimum for barrelling waves. Onshore waves tend to be messy and not much good for anything but fun, frothy surfs. It's a common misconception with the public that strong onshore winds mean good waves. However, explaining why long-travelled swell created by wind/fetch/duration in an offshore storm creates better surf takes a while – maybe it's easier just to give them a copy of this book.

Another influence on the waves is the tide. Every knowledgeable surfer keeps a hawk-eye on the tides. The boffins have studied it and the surfers agree that waves can be bigger on a pushing tide. One hour before high being the peak.

The generation and propagation of waves is a fascinating subject and the science of it is well worth looking into. The people that are at the cutting edge of wave pool technology certainly have. Whilst the new concept of Wave Gardens are fun and Kelly Slater's wave pool looks incredible, it's worth thinking about how, even with all the knowledge, science, engineering skill and money at our disposal, we still struggle to replicate what nature does every day so effortlessly.

NORTHERN CALIFORNIA. PHOTO: MARCUS PALADINO

PORTHLEVEN, ENGLAND. PHOTO: MIKE LACEY

PORTHLEVEN, ENGLAND. PHOTO: MIKE LACEY

AUSTRALIA. PHOTO: JOSH TABONE

PORTUGAL. PHOTO: HELIO ANTONIO

THE BIGGEST
WAVE _

When wind just isn't quite enough

Much is made of surfing the biggest wave: the elusive quest to ride a 100-foot record breaker. Even though Nazaré in Portugal is scraping that realm, the biggest recorded wind-generated waves are open ocean behemoths found in huge storms. Not the photogenic or surfable kind. But as you might suspect, the biggest waves on Earth aren't due to a puff of wind...

Lituya Bay, in deepest Alaska, was the scene of the world's highest recorded wave. As a young surfer/geologist this annoyed me. You see, it wasn't a proper wave, not a mighty ocean swell from an explosively cyclogenic 'perfect' storm, not even a tsunami, the ungodly offspring produced by tectonic plates having a tiff. It was a hoax, a one-in-a-million shot, an aberration of nature. Originally it was also misunderstood.

American geologists first noticed something strange at Lituya during the early fifties, whilst surveying for oil. Normally the primordial forest reaches right down to the shoreline, but in the bay they found an unusual demarcation. At about 150 metres above sea level the mature growth ceased and below it much younger trees sprouted. It was as if some unknown force had just wiped the slate clean and nature started afresh. The geologists were stumped.

In an early attempt at scientific cross-pollination they took samples from trees around the trim line and had the tree ring section analysed. The results were conclusive; a powerful force had surged into the forest, leaving the surviving mature trees on the edge of the tree line badly bruised. The only feasible explanation was that a wave up to a height of 150 metres above sea level had hit the forest. This was completely outside the box – a wave the height of a fifty-storey building?

The most recent and well-known tsunami at the time had hit Hilo, Hawaii, in 1946, causing mass devastation and killing 100 people. It came from a sea floor quake thousands of kilometres away, yet whilst being phenomenally destructive the wave was only ten-metres high. The geologists knew that normal earthquake-generated tsunamis are inherently limited in size by the disturbance that caused them. Meaning a ten-metre displacement of the sea floor results in approximately a ten-metre high wave on the surface.

The geologists left Lituya Bay in 1953 completely mystified, having found no oil and no explanation for what they had seen. It was a mere five years before they got their answer. Another huge wave hit Lituya Bay and this time there were witnesses. On 9 July 1958, three fishing vessels were moored in the calm haven of Lituya when, at around ten o'clock in the evening the tranquillity was broken by an unearthly rumbling coming from the mountains at the head of the bay. A minute later a monstrous wall of water bore down on the boats. Paralysed with fear, the crew of one boat watched as 40 fathoms of anchor chain paid out before snapping like a piece of string. Amazingly that one boat surfed the wave over the treetops and came back to rest in the bay, but the other two craft were washed out to sea and smashed into kindling. One two-man crew died yet the others somehow survived.

THE GREAT WAVE OFF KANAGAWA.
WOODBLOCK PRINT : HOKUSAI

Dawn revealed a scene of devastation: Trees and soil stripped away leaving bare bedrock up to 520 metres above sea level. Surveying by plane the next day, one of the original geologists spotted something different at the head of the bay. On closer inspection it became apparent that a massive section of the mountain had fallen off into the bay. This time it was obvious what had happened – a massive cataclysmic landslide. It soon became apparent that the Lituya wave was indirectly caused by a strong earthquake after all, it was the quake that had induced the rock fall.

It is a commonly known fact that throwing a stone into a pool of water makes waves. Mass makes waves. So drop ninety million tonnes of rock into a sea loch and the same effect is observed. The wave that resulted was, at the time, taller than all of the skyscrapers that existed; even today only two scratch over that height. This got the scientists of the world thinking. Why did this happen? Could it happen anywhere else and, most pressingly, in a populated area?

Sea floor surveys in the sixties, the same ones that helped confirm the theory of tectonics, showed that this was a common occurrence around one particular kind of location: the large volcanic island. Of which, as surfers, we know plenty:

Hawaii, Reunion, Madeira, the Azores, the Canaries – the list goes on. As these islands grew (or, in the case of Hawaii's Big Island, grow) by successive eruptions of lava and volcanic rubble, they build an inherently unstable structure prone to periodic collapse. Anyone who has been to Madeira and wondered why the village of Jardim do Mar sits on a relatively flat coastal platform when the bulk of the island is surrounded by steep cliff, here's your answer: It's the top of a massive landslide and the scoop shape in the cliffs above the village show where the material came from.

When the scientists started looking they found evidence for past collapses everywhere. In Hawaii the sea floor is littered with vast chunks of rock that have fallen. Eighty thousand years ago Cape Verde suffered a massive collapse and, most recently, Reunion Island in the Indian Ocean lost some volume a mere 4,000 years ago. All these events would have generated huge waves, now known as mega-tsunamis. These waves would have hit the west coast of America, North Africa and West Australia respectively. There's even evidence in Somerset of a medieval wave reaching a mile inland, as a result of a collapse off Ireland. All the scientific enquiry into the theory of mega-tsunamis

was devastatingly verified on Boxing Day 2004 with the Indian Ocean disaster, and then again in Japan in 2011, when the resulting chaos was captured on rolling news.

The problem with mega-tsunamis is the huge wavelength. Even the biggest normal wind-generated waves have a wavelength in the order of tens of metres. Mega-tsunamis have a wavelength measured in kilometres. When they approach land they don't just break, they engulf. The huge wall of water at the leading edge of the wave doesn't just break on the coast, the whole wave surges many miles inland as chillingly demonstrated in the helicopter footage from Japan.

Big earthquakes, landslides, sea floor collapse and meteorites can all cause these kinds of waves. It's not just in the realm of Hollywood sci-fi films or scientific 'what if?'. We've witnessed the wrath of the most violent waves on the planet and can only hope we don't experience another one.

USGS

TAHITI. PHOTO: BEN THOUARD

VANCOUVER ISLAND, CANADA. PHOTO: MARCUS PALADINO

TOFINO, CANADA. PHOTO: MARCUS PALADINO

"
FOR ME, A GOOD WAVE PHOTO HAS TO
BE SOMETHING INCREDIBLY UNIQUE
- WHETHER IT BE WEIRD LIGHT/
WEATHER COMBINATIONS, A FRESH
ANGLE, OR JUST SIMPLY ONE OF THOSE
OUTRAGEOUS 'ONCE IN A BLUE MOON'
MOMENTS WHERE YOU'RE LUCKY
ENOUGH TO BE AIMING YOUR CAMERA
IN THE RIGHT DIRECTION.
"

- JOSH TABONE

AUSTRALIA. PHOTO: JOSH TABONE

CALIFORNIA, PHOTO: CHRIS BURKARD

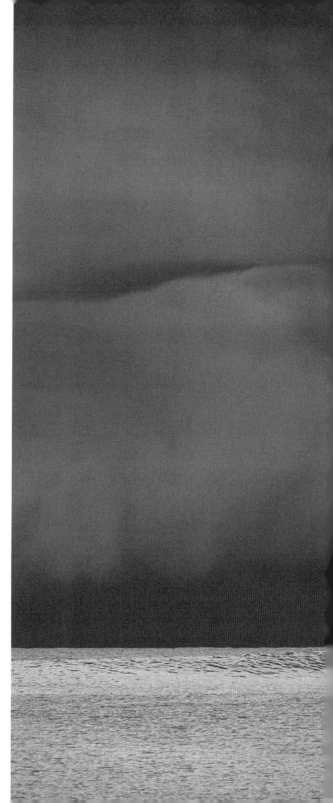

"

I THINK A GOOD WAVE PHOTO
CONSISTS OF MOOD, COLOURS AND
CONTRAST. PLUS SOME MOVEMENT AS
WELL. PERFECT SUNNY IMAGES ARE
GREAT, BUT DARK IMAGES CONVEY
MORE OF A STORY.

"

- RODD OWEN

INDONESIA. PHOTO: RODD OWEN

THE STATE OF
WAVE PHOTOGRAPHY_

It's easier than ever to take swell photos

Since Tom Blake built the first wooden water housing for a camera in 1930, surf photographers have always shot images of the stunning saline sculptures they're immersed in.

After all, capturing nature's beauty at its most fleeting and ephemeral is part of the art. Empty wave shots appeal to anyone with an eye for colour and form.

Not having a surfer in the frame means that you can escape the sporting niche of surf photography and the shot isn't dated by fashion or logos.

Take Clark Little; he's become a global icon with his wave photos and has inspired a legion of acolytes that seek digital salvation in the shorebreak.

Ocean photography is also easier and cheaper than it ever has been now that there's no need for thousands of pounds worth of fancy gear. A few hundred pounds on a decent GoPro and you can get killer wave shots yourself.

Shooting empty waves is also easier than surf photography. You don't need a willing surfer to work with and frame, and without someone heading towards you on a fibreglass missile at 20mph it's also a lot safer. Depending on if you're shooting shorebreak or not. Shorebreak of any size is a hell of a loosener for the joints.

If you're into becoming a surf photographer then shooting waves is the ideal way to get comfortable in one of the hardest studios there is to master.

Sure, there are plenty of surf photographers out there already, along with a dwindling number of magazines and surf brand opportunities to support them financially. But shooting waves is a purer pursuit. You create a body of work that can be sold as prints and canvasses, not to mention looking rad on your Instagram. Wave shots are timeless. They're works of art. Nature frozen at 1000th of a second. Never to be repeated. Not forgetting as a wave artist you shoot for yourself – not for money. It's your vision; your interpretation of the meeting of water, wind and light. So if anyone else digs them, especially to the point of wanting your image on their wall, then it's just a bonus.

It's exciting times in the medium of photography as cameras become ever cheaper, smaller, better and – the most recent breakthrough – more sensitive. You can shoot before the sun comes up and after it goes down. Hell, you can even shoot the Northern Lights these days without a noisy image. The potential for creativity is vast. Waves happen from two inches to twenty feet all over the world. You can create art with them if you desire. One other awesome thing about shooting waves: they don't need to be surfable. Mutant near dry slabs with four lips look awesome, but won't be troubled by riders. Similarly, perfect six-inch peelers are awesome to shoot yet not to surf, so you can still be in the brine having fun. Body surfing is the purest form of wave riding and being a surf photographer means you'll get pretty good at it.

HOSSEGOR, FRANCE. PHOTO: LAURENT PUJOL

BLUE BOWLS, MALDIVES. PHOTO: ROGER SHARP

THE RIGHT, WESTERN AUSTRALIA. PHOTO: TRENT SLATTER

"

A GOOD WAVE PHOTO PULLS THE
VIEWER IN, IN THE WAY THAT YOU MIND
SURF THAT THING TO DEATH. THE WAVE
ITSELF MIGHT BE UNMAKEABLE, BUT
THAT 1/1000 SECOND FROZEN MOMENT
TELLS US SOMETHING DIFFERENT.
THERE ARE A MILLION TINY DETAILS
AND SINCE IT'S SOMETHING UNIQUE,
WHICH WILL NEVER EVER HAPPEN IN
THE EXACT SAME WAY AGAIN, IT'S JUST
MINDBLOWING TO WATCH.

"

- TIMO JARVINEN

SUNSET REEF, SOUTH AFRICA. PHOTO: ALAN VAN GYSEN

MIKADO, MALDIVES. PHOTO: ROGER SHARP

CARIBBEAN. PHOTO: CHRIS BURKARD

"

I THINK TO MAKE A GOOD WAVE PHOTO,
YOU REALLY NEED TO THINK ABOUT
THE LIGHT, AS LIGHT WOULD CREATE A
REFLECTION OR AN EFFECT THAT WILL
PLAY WITH THE SURFACE OF THE WATER
TO ADD A GREAT WOW TO JUST AN
EMPTY WAVE PHOTO. OF COURSE THE
SPOT AND HOW THE WAVE BREAKS IS
ALSO IMPORTANT, BUT I THINK LIGHT IS
AS IMPORTANT, IF NOT MORE, THAN THE
SHAPE OF THE WAVE.

"

- BEN THOUARD

PLASTIC BEACH_

The waves and oceans are in big trouble

The only thing that should be in our waves is salt water and the marine life that calls them home. Sadly, this is increasingly not the case. The oceans and our wave-rich playground are under a myriad of threats from pollution of all kinds.

On the grand scale, climate change could lead to the sea level rising, which may stop some waves breaking. If it all goes really wrong, even the storm systems that generate our waves might change. If the Arctic keeps warming up and the Atlantic currents shut down, no one knows what will happen for sure. So, in Northern Europe at least, the worst-case scenario is a frozen, waveless future. Not fun.

On a local level, ocean pollution, especially from plastics, is a massive problem all over the world. Waves should not be full of shopping bags and ear bud sticks. Beaches shouldn't be littered with needles and junk. We shouldn't even be talking about trash islands afloat in our seas.

We asked writer and environmentalist Martin Dorey, from #2minutebeachclean, for some pointers on what we can all do about it:

What's the worst threat to our waves?

We are. All of us. So many of us. That's it really. If we continue to consume without a thought for the future, all we'll have left is plastic strewn beaches and dead, trash-filled oceans. The waves will still be there but it's not going to feel good, is it?

What can we all personally do about it?

Everyone can make a difference. You just have to go a little bit out of your way to do it sometimes. Buy a keep cup. Use a refillable water bottle. Do a #2minutebeachclean each time you hit the water. Join a beach clean. Think carefully about how you consume.

We also need to recycle more, buy less stuff, repair what breaks, refuse single use plastics, think more locally, explore in a sustainable way, stop blaming the developing world for litter problems and get on with clearing up what we see – each and every day. As surfers we have a duty to our homelands and playgrounds. As surfers, consumers and travellers we have power and presence. If we can't use it for good then what's the point in having it?

What do companies need to work on fixing?

Every company, not just in the surf industry, needs to look at the entire life cycle of its products. They need to design the end of their product's life as well as its conception. They need to think about how it could be repaired or re-used or recycled. That should also be law. Which means that supermarkets selling lettuces in trays need to start taking those trays back, or stop using them at all, or at the very least make sure that they can be recycled easily and locally.

Brands need to give us choices to do the right thing. Currently many of them don't. If I buy a shirt from an online retailer it comes in plastic I don't want. They need to stop that now. They need to stop relying on plastics and start thinking about the future. How can a surf brand that takes itself seriously, and gets its money from people enjoying the ocean, not be environmental to the very core? It still baffles me that it is possible...

Get involved with the campaign on Instagram: @2minutebeachclean

RIGHT **INDONESIA. PHOTO: ZAK NOYLE/A-FRAME**
FOLLOWING SPREAD **EDDYSTONE ROCK. PHOTO: ANDREW CHISHOLM**

THE PIRATE ISLES, MADAGASCAR. PHOTO: ALAN VAN GYSEN

PIPELINE, HAWAII. PHOTO: JOSH TABONE

NOTES_

THE PHOTOGRAPHERS TELL THE STORIES BEHIND THEIR SHOTS

COOK ISLANDS
PHOTO: JOSH TABONE

I went to the Cook Islands hoping to score a week of waves with some of my mates. This was day one of our trip - on one coast it was 10-12ft with onshore winds and on the other it was 4-6ft with some of the most perfect A-frames I've ever seen. After a long walk out, dodging urchins, you're greeted with a hairy rock jump into raw Pacific power. Two sessions later we were cooked. The rest of the week was rubbish and we almost went mad, circling the island on mopeds and playing cards. Definitely one of the most fickle places I have ever been!

TAHITI
PHOTO: BEN THOUARD

This is another wave in Tahiti that rarely works and which is really heavy; it's pretty much a close out on certain days. That day was pretty clean and I loved how long and clean the wave was, making it look like a wall and the spray from the lip creating a rainbow.

SOUTHERN NEW SOUTH WALES, AUSTRALIA
PHOTO: RODD OWEN

The cobra-looking slab is truly a freak of nature. Peaking and standing up then finally hitting the ledge on the inside, it makes for spectacular images when the conditions align.

INDONESIA
PHOTO: TIMO JARVINEN

This bommie is located near Lagundri. That day Nias was chest-high perfection, but this beast was throwing 12ft bombs, going mad in front of dry reef. Some folk call it the heaviest wave in Indo. I don't think identifying it has any kind of an effect on how crowded it'll become... it's that heavy that it'll take care of itself when it comes to overcrowding. That day Aritz Aranburu, Indar Unaune and Leo Fioravanti tackled the beast and it was an epic session for sure. It's as remote as anything so if things go down, getting an injury would have serious consequences.

AUSTRALIA
PHOTO: JOSH TABONE

This photo is from one of the biggest swells I've seen on the east coast. I trekked about an hour through some thick Aussie bush to get to the cliff edge at this particular spot. Such a breathtaking view, over-looking the beach, whilst having a few coldies at sunset. Watching the monstrous waves was nice too!

THURSO, SCOTLAND
PHOTO: ROGER SHARP

A rare empty one makes it through the pack unmolested at Thurso East. When it comes to pretty waves TE is up there with the best of them. A world-class gem that's fickle and freezing, but a beauty when it does actually break. It's just hard to motivate yourself into a wet, cold wetsuit when the car dash tells you it's -2C outside. But when it's pumping you've got to do it.

GUMS, HAWAII
PHOTO: TIMO JARVINEN

I swam out to Pipe early with Alain Riou; he had a bomb and then on the next one he broke his board and went in. I stayed out as Dorian had just paddled out. He went deep and I knew something was gonna go down, it was big first reef stuff. Then for some reason I turned and looked towards Ehukai and saw this crazy wedge coming in. There's actually a bodyboarder attempting to paddle out, but this one regulated him pretty badly. It was a beautiful thing to witness; it breaks into a foot of water and is one of the worst places on the North Shore to be when things go wrong.

PIPELINE, HAWAII
PHOTO: JOSH TABONE

From the winter of 2016. The first two days of February were some of the best Pipeline I've ever seen! Sun up, to sun down! Koa Rothman is a definite stand out at Pipe. He got a few this particular afternoon, all crazy hollow pits. He's probably had thousands of these in his lifetime, if not more!

JEFFREY'S BAY, SOUTH AFRICA
PHOTO: ALAN VAN GYSEN

Since the dawn of it's discovery, the groomed, reeling perfection of Indian Ocean lines, birthed in the adjacent Atlantic has enthralled and lured in surfers of every race, gender, religion, culture and class. And it's thanks to line-ups likes these that dreams of surfing its tapered, speedy walls have been sparked and nurtured worlds away, long before most surfers even step off the plane into South Africa. And like Africa, it's raw, wild and mysterious, and promises adventure and excitement.

KAI LENNY, MAVERICKS, CALIFORNIA
PHOTO: BASTIEN BONNARME

Kai Lenny is the very essence of the much abused term 'waterman'. If it can be used to ride waves he can ride it better than most. This is him at an all time day at Mavericks, one of the most dangerous and revered waves in the world.

TEAHUPO'O, TAHITI
PHOTO: BEN THOUARD

Another image from my underwater portfolio. I love how crystal the water looks.

BASS STRAIT, AUSTRALIA
PHOTO: ANDREW SHIELD

This beach break is unique in that it's one of very few north facing beaches in Australia that still gets waves. Giant Southern Ocean swells wrap around both sides of the island and form perfect peaks. They look like the type of waves kids draw on their schoolbooks ... do schools still have pens and notebooks?

TEAHUPO'O, TAHITI
PHOTO: BEN THOUARD

This is Dion Atkinson in Tahiti during the WSL CT event in 2014. The contest period saw a run of two huge swells hitting Tahiti that was probably the best paddle swell ever seen here. Dion was just amazed by how good the conditions were.

SCOTLAND
PHOTO: ROGER SHARP

The wave known as Tens is a short, shallow, slurping, brutal slab. It doesn't like to be ridden. It is however a fantastic place to shoot wave studies – as its warped physics produces all manner of crazy. Here's one that actually looks surfable.

TAHITI
PHOTO: BEN THOUARD

Another lucky moment that explains being in the right place at the right time. As the storm approached, I tried to take advantage of the last few minutes I had before the storm hit the coast. I stepped back a little from the spot and decided to shoot it pulled back to give a lonely feeling of this wave in this situation.

TAHITI
PHOTO: BEN THOUARD

This is John John Florence on a special wave during a special day in Tahiti! Probably the best conditions I've seen out there. John caught this wave paddling on his 5'10".

LOFOTEN ISLANDS, NORWAY
PHOTO: CHRIS BURKARD

One of many unridden waves in a magical bay nestled in the Lofoten Islands of Norway.

TEAHUPO'O, TAHITI
PHOTO: BEN THOUARD

This is Anthony Walsh at Teahupo'o during a day off from the WSL Tahiti CT event. This is one of my favourite underwater photos – I've been working on this angle for a very long time now and I'm glad how everything linked up together.

ACEH PROVINCE INDONESIA
PHOTO: ANDREW SHIELD

I'd always wanted to go check out this wave because it looked longer than your typical Indo reef break and great for line-up shots. It's actually bigger than it looks – on this day the waves up the top of the reef were easily eight feet. We shot it from the water in the morning and then in the arvo we hiked through some mangroves and across sharp shallow reef to a tower that had only recently been put up. In most western countries you wouldn't be able to get anywhere near a tower like this, let alone climb it. It would be surrounded by fencing and barbed wire. Not in Indo though.

HAWAIIAN SURFING SKETCH EARLY 1800S
ILLUSTRATION: BERNICE PAUAHI BISHOP MUSEUM

Sketches made by European explorers in the early 1800s. These give us an insight into the cultural significance of surfing to Pacific Island life.

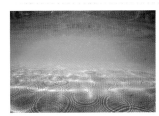

AUSTRALIA
PHOTO: JOSH TABONE

From a special little cove, near my house in Australia. The very beginning of a sun shower... One of those moments.

NEW SOUTH WALES, AUSTRALIA
PHOTO: RODD OWEN

One of the biggest south swells to hit New South Wales in the past ten years. Throwing early morning shadows down over the lip. This particular swell lasted four days straight with perfect winds the entire run.

EDDYSTONE ROCK, TASMANIA
PHOTO: ANDREW CHISHOLM

We departed the wharf around three in the morning to be out at Eddystone Rock just before sunrise. After a few cans the night before the rough trip out seemed to make the journey take longer. The level of excitement was pretty high as near perfect conditions unfolded before us. The light bouncing off the white water really made this image and the pillar rock just speaks for itself.

NEW SOUTH WALES, AUSTRALIA
PHOTO: JOSH TABONE

Some of the largest and roundest, sand-bottom barrels I've ever seen in Australia. This day actually reminded me of Mexico. The water colour, the power and the consistency. When the waves are clean and perfect like this, I love shooting more pulled back to give the viewer a little something to mind surf. You can also see how god-damn windy it was out there!

DUNES, SOUTH AFRICA
PHOTO: ALAN VAN GYSEN

Africa's Puerto Escondido, The Dunes is everything you could ever want in a wave. Split peaks up and down a perfect white sand beach, with an almost year-round predominant offshore wind and exposure to every ripple that is sent from the 'Roaring 40s' from anywhere across the mighty south Atlantic Ocean. Barrels for breakfast, lunch and dinner!

DONKEY BAY, NAMIBIA
PHOTO: ALAN VAN GYSEN

The world's most perfect wave. Donkey, aka 'Skeleton' Bay breaking over 2.1km of shallow Namib sand, with every possibility on offer of your best wave ever ridden. Just watch out for the 2.1km walk back. 10 waves equals 21km's of walking!

PORTHTOWAN, CORNWALL
PHOTO: ROGER SHARP

The perfect colours of early summer in Cornwall when the visibilty is stunning and the Atlantic shows off its kinder side. Oli Adams enjoys a solo session.

AUSTRALIA
PHOTO: RODD OWEN

We discovered this wave 50km off the coast by pure luck, whilst running out of fuel on our jetski. Returning the day after was one of the most memorable sessions of my life. Heaviest wave I've ever seen or heard by a mile.

OCCY'S LEFT, INDONESIA
PHOTO: RODD OWEN

One of the bigger Indonesian swells last season; I was lucky enough to stay near the wave for two weeks. Truly incredible setup with not a soul surfing besides us for the entire swell.

CORNWALL
PHOTO: ROGER SHARP

Longships lighthouse off Land's End in Cornwall during a huge winter storm. The lighthouse is 35 metres high so that gives some sense of the incredible energy unloading. Waves aren't always pretty... Sometimes it's all about the shock and awe. Shooting in a fierce gale, with heaps of sea spray in the air, was a real challenge. Especially as this was shot on an old 800mm manual focus lens.

TAHITI
PHOTO: BEN THOUARD

The photo that really pushed me onto shooting empty waves. I shot this photo in 2011 and it definitely marked the beginning of a long quest.

WESTERN AUSTRALIA
PHOTO: RYAN MILLER

Jack Robinson as shot from my dearly departed DJI Mavic Pro. It had a short but productive life. Scoring a covershot on Carve and some other great shots. The day after this session it couldn't fight its way back to shore against the strong Margies offshores and it ended up landing itself in the Indian Ocean.

EAST COAST, SOUTH AFRICA
PHOTO: ALAN VAN GYSEN

Not as consistent as Jeffrey's Bay perhaps, nor as busy, but this spot – like Bruce's Beauties – is just as perfect and lined up on the right swell as any of the many incredible, quieter right points of South Africa.

KIRRA, AUSTRALIA
PHOTO: ANDREW SHIELD

Coolangatta has dozens of high-rise apartment buildings right on the beach. When I'm in the water I'm always looking up to see which one would offer a good vantage point for line-up shots. This one behind Kirra is ideal because it allows you to get the famous Kirra eagle sculpture in the shot as well. This day was the tail end of a pumping five day swell and it was very uncrowded, which is super rare for Kirra.

ANCHOVIES, SOLOMON ISLANDS
PHOTO: ANDREW SHIELD

The Pacific Ocean north swell season runs from October to April. Everyone knows how good Hawaii gets at this time of year, but there are literally thousands of other destinations right across the Pacific that cop swell from those huge winter storms. On this trip the boys were surprised at the size and power of this wave, and after copping a bit of a beating for a couple of days we motored out on this day and it was a much more pleasant 4-6 foot. And not another soul in sight. Just love the, 'Are you kidding me?' hand gesture.

MAVERICKS, CALIFORNIA
PHOTO: BASTIEN BONNARME

The bathymetry of Mavericks is fascinating and worth a web search. The short version is: huge Pacific swell lines born from storms spinning off the north of Japan into the Aleutians make their way thousand of miles and rage against the shore of California in spectacular fashion. And hence are always well documented.

TAHITI
PHOTO: BEN THOUARD

I remember cruising on my jet ski when I saw this little wave breaking on dry reef. It's not a surf spot, it's just a close out on dry reef, but it looked so perfect to me that I decided to jump in and I shot for two hours. It was one of those days when you just need to be there at the right time.

THE AFRICAN KIRRA, MOZAMBIQUE
PHOTO: ALAN VAN GYSEN

The rarity of spots like this is what makes this wave so special and unique. Sand, swell, direction and tide all have to come together in the perfect mix to produce the goods. These gems existed for a about four hours on this historic day, and then the ocean went flat, literally.

LANCE'S LEFT, INDONESIA
PHOTO: ANDREW SHIELD

This is shot from the Kingfisher surf camp. All the rooms have a great view of the surf, but I liked the shot from this room because of the water in the foreground. Lance's Left is overshadowed a bit buy the more famous right around the corner (Lance's Right/HTs/Hollow Trees) but the left is also a great wave. I saw it on a huge swell in 2015 and it looked a lot like giant Cloudbreak – 10-15 foot but handling and really perfect.

AUSTRALIA
PHOTO: RODD OWEN

Another outer reef draining up with a rainbow overhead. The ledge on this reef goes from 300m to 2m directly under this wave. A super heavy and also deceivingly perfect slab.

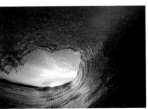

THE BOOM, NICARAGUA
PHOTO: ROGER SHARP

One of the most perfect A-frame beachbreaks anywhere. The Boom only works an hour either side of high tide so it's a swine to catch, as the wind goes onshore at 10:30am like clockwork. If you've got your maths right and are there with the early morning tides then you'll be in heaven. A couple of coffees in the half light, check the plume from the volcano is blowing offshore, run down the beach and jump in for sunrise. Then, after a few hours fun, back for brekkie and a long lunchtime hammock siesta session with a good book and a cerveza or three.

TELOS, INDONESIA
PHOTO: ANDREW SHIELD

This was shot around the corner from Telo Island Lodge. The wave is a pretty long, fun right that breaks right in front of the lodge. To get this shot I enlisted the help of one the local guys and we carried a six-foot-high step ladder through the waist-deep water of this channel, so as to get a bit of height to see over the reef and the whitewater in front of the wave.

RILEYS, IRELAND
PHOTO: LAURENT PUJOL

Shane Dorian made the long trip from Hawaii to Ireland to explore the coldwater scene. He scored Aileens and Rileys as good as they get, which is so lucky it's not even funny. It's a hectic place to shoot as it's so shallow, but the channel is just big enough to hang in without getting destroyed.

THE POINTS, AUSTRALIA
PHOTO: ANDREW CHISHOLM

Just over the hill there may be another wave; I remember first surfing these waves a long time ago, by myself, and there was always another set up you could see just over the hill. The level of excitement was always high when these waves were on as they are a bit of a rarity. I sat out on the windswept hill for a couple hours with no one about and finally a break in the clouds and a four-wave set just happened to coincide at the same time. I could not believe my luck! For all that to fall into place was bordering on a miracle, plus the crow flying through as well!

TAHITI
PHOTO: BEN THOUARD

This wave is a gnarly slab that the bodyboarders surf. It does not work that often but I remember swimming seven hours straight that day, it was so intense, I just couln't leave the spot.

IRELAND
PHOTO: ROGER SHARP

Perfect form at a wave that appears in videos and magazines frequently but is never named. It's been known as Kelpies, Out Front, Mikeys and many more. It's one of the best places in Europe to shoot watershots. Even though it's very shallow, it's relatively safe. That said, get caught inside on the right on a solid day and you won't need to visit a chiropractor for a while.

DESERT POINT, INDONESIA
PHOTO: ANDREW CHISHOLM

Have you ever been to a place you have read and dreamed about for your entire surfing life and finally had the opportunity to go there? I remember four places specifically. The North Shore of Hawaii, Shipsterns, Snapper Rocks and Desert Point. The road in was pretty rough over the hills just before getting to the wave, but as we rolled into the surf side village I just remember this perfectly groomed set coming in standing up on the reef and barrelling perfectly the whole way through to 'The Grower'. This I will never forget!

MALLORCA, SPAIN
PHOTO: DAMIAN DAVILA

It's amazing the images you can capture whilst messing around in the Mediterranean shore break at sunset.

TAHITI
PHOTO: BEN THOUARD

A nasty west bowl at Teahupo'o on a really west swell, combined with a technical shooting mode, created this night effect.

CYCLOPS, WESTERN AUSTRALIA
PHOTO: TRENT SLATTER

I had just bough a new 4WD ($4000) and was at the pub with my best mate having a cheap steak on a Wednesday night. We were just looking at the charts and next minute we're doing a 12hr mission, laughing and having the time of our life. We arrived at sunrise and went straight out and started pushing our comfort zones. We went in for a feed and I swapped SD cards. Going back out we got a bit too cheeky and ended up losing a camera. Back on land we packed up our gear and drove straight home minus a camera but still had the contents as I'd swapped cards!

PORTHLEVEN, ENGLAND
PHOTO: MIKE LACEY

Underwater World is one I took in May 2016 in Porthleven. It was one of the clearest days I had seen and full of life on the reef, so I spent the whole session just getting underwater shots and this one was one of my favourites. I love the seaweed that frames the wave and shows the movement of the water.

NORTHERN CALIFORNIA
PHOTO: MARCUS PALADINO

This spot is only a few miles out of town and is probably one of the most user-friendly set ups to get barrelled on. Good luck getting a set wave though, the old crusty locals don't take kindly to strangers around here. Seems like only a select few surf this wave on a regular basis, and they've been doing so since they were groms. So an unfamiliar surfer sticks out like a sore thumb.

PORTHLEVEN, ENGLAND
PHOTO: MIKE LACEY

Porthole is one of my favourites from 2016, as I wanted to get a shot that frames the clock like this for so long.

SANTA CRUZ, CALIFORNIA
PHOTO: MARCUS PALADINO

This ain't no wave pool, but I wouldn't be surprised if Kelly Slater was inspired by this spot right in the heart of Santa Cruz. Despite being in the middle of town, you would probably drive past this beach and not even notice the kegging tubes below. Some locals are so dedicated to their wave that despite the diverse coast, they won't surf anywhere else (or even at all) if it's breaking.

AUSTRALIA
PHOTO: JOSH TABONE

This is a view surfers never get bored of. If the water is clear, always have a mask in your kit to witness this hydrodynamic spectacle.

ST IVES BAY, CORNWALL
PHOTO: MIKE LACEY

One of the most perfect sessions I've had in Cornwall and we had it like this for five days! So many of my friends were away on surf trips wishing they were back in Cornwall. It was the most insane week.

PORTUGAL
PHOTO: HELIO ANTONIO

Water photographers need to work together to play nice. But sometimes the other guys make for some foreground interest.

WESTERN AUSTRALIA
PHOTO: TRENT SLATTER

This was three days into a four day 10-20ft swell with offshore winds, simply unheard of, and possibly a joke. The line-up had thinned out and the light opened up to possibly make the most dream-like conditions and I happened to get lucky with a few frames thanks to Russell Ord's tips. I feel like he handed me a gift with his advice and I'm forever grateful. After getting back to land and not eating for six hours I opened a bag of oranges and they where like the most amazing thing I'd ever tasted. Each time when I now eat oranges it takes me instantly to that moment.

THE GREAT WAVE OFF KANAGAWA
WOODBLOCK PRINT : HOKUSAI

The world famous image from incredible Japanese artist Hokusai, depicts an enormous wave threatening fishing boats off the coast of the prefecture of Kanagawa. While sometimes assumed to be a tsunami, the wave is more likely to be a large rogue wave. As in all the images in the series, it depicts the area around Mount Fuji under particular conditions, and the mountain itself appears in the background.

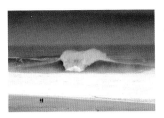

NAZARÉ, PORTUGAL
PHOTO: HELIO ANTONIO

The biggest ridable waves in the world break at Nazaré; it also works when it's two foot. It's the in-between sizes when the really crazy stuff happens. As a beachbreak it has so many moods. Endlessly fascinating to shoot.

TAHITI
PHOTO: BEN THOUARD

The same wave in Tahiti that works rarely and is really heavy; it's pretty much a closeout on certain days but that day was pretty clean. I loved how long and clean the wave was, making it look like a wall.

VANCOUVER ISLAND, CANADA
PHOTO: MARCUS PALADINO

This spot is a remote location that's only accessible by local knowledge. It only breaks like this a handful of times a year, but when it does Pete Devries is always the first person in the water. This morning was no exception, he went wave for wave with his best friends from sun up till sundown.

TOFINO, CANADA
PHOTO: MARCUS PALADINO

I stood on the beach and took photos for eight hours straight, it was one of those perfect winter days. Sun was shining, waves were pumping and everyone was out. When this one came through I couldn't believe no-one was in position to catch it. While mind surfing, I caught the wave of the day.

PIPELINE, HAWAII
PHOTO: JOSH TABONE

Can you believe this thing went unridden?! This monster of a wave actually rolled through between the semis and final at the 2016 Volcom Pipe comp. You could hear Kelly Slater scream in agony after being in position for this but unable to take it as the heat hadn't started yet. I took this from the check spot, with my camera nestled inside my water-housing... I was actually waiting for the comp to finish so I could swim out. The amount of times I've taken usable photos from within my housing (on land) is strange.

P-PASS, MICRONESIA
PHOTO: ANDREW SHIELD

P-Pass has become the favourite wave of just about everyone I've ever gone over there with. I was in the channel on a jet ski that day and scored some great shots of Jay Davies and Mikey Wright (pictured). I went across the channel to try to get some of the boats in the foreground and Mikey got this one. It was probably one of the best waves of the session and I though I'd blown it by being back behind the boats, but this shot has become a bit of an iconic pic.

AUSTRALIA
PHOTO: JOSH TABONE

I'll never forget this day... The waves were absolutely cooking, and a massive pod of dolphins – easily 50 or more – were cruising the line-up, taking waves and frolicking around the peak. I swam for a few hours, snapped this one and went in to make lunch. Soon after, another large pod approached the peak. A large bunch of them all swam for the next wave that come through. It was pretty wild, they were jumping, leaping and dancing towards the shoreline, and some even hung on right to the channel.

CALIFORNIA
PHOTO: CHRIS BURKARD

Central California isn't necessarily known for its consistency of surf, however, when all the conditions align, it can be pretty magical.

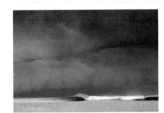

INDONESIA
PHOTO: RODD OWEN

Perfect afternoon lines at a rarely surfed location in Sumatra. The evening storm front swung the winds to offshore, six-foot perfect rights until dark.

HOSSEGOR, FRANCE
PHOTO: LAURENT PUJOL

Jeremy Flores taking time out from the world tour to work on the trickiest way of shooting surf photos. It takes a lot of nerve to agree to a surf photographer to tow in behind you and hope for the best. When it works out the results are sublime.

BLUE BOWLS, MALDIVES
PHOTO: ROGER SHARP

Drones have opened up a whole new world in wave photography. The 'angle of god' was once the preserve of photog's rich enough to hire a helicopter. Now you can fit a drone in your pocket. So really far-flung places, like the southern atolls of the Maldives, down near the equator, can be shot in new ways. I just love the colours in this and how you can see the dynamics of the reef and swell interacting.

THE RIGHT, WESTERN AUSTRALIA
PHOTO: TRENT SLATTER

Every wave since this one is compared to Dean Morrisons, as The Right was unseen by the masses before this session. My main camera didn't want to work that day so I was shooting off my back-up and the frame rate isn't as quick, so I was stoked with what I ended up with, even though eventually we went for an unplanned swim and the camera stopped working. A kind lady back onshore had some rice and a day later it worked again.

NIAS, INDONESIA
PHOTO: TIMO JARVINEN

This day saw 15 guys in the line-up, but when solid sets came through there were not that many willing takers. This drop is black belt stuff in my book and definitely something I wasn't prepared to see when we left home. Leo has become a world class tube pig and it felt insane to witness this day from the channel. The wave did exactly the same all day and it made me wonder when was the last time I witnessed something like it – no motion sickness, no sea breeze, nothing … just perfection from sunrise to sunset.

TOFINO, CANADA
PHOTO: MARCUS PALADINO

The south side of this beach break in Tofino is often overlooked and underrated. More often than not, it's too small, being protected by the surrounding islands. Most locals choose to surf down the beach in lieu of more swell and size. But when everything lines up and you know what the magic tide is, I can guarantee you'll be the only person out there.

SUNSET REEF, SOUTH AFRICA
PHOTO: ALAN VAN GYSEN

The lesser publicised African big wave spot – Sunset Reef – might not be as famous as Dungeons across the bay, but where it lacks in international fame it certainly makes up for in perfection, raw power and ease of access. Just the way the locals like it.

MIKADO, MALDIVES
PHOTO: ROGER SHARP

Another drone shot that's as much about the crazy reef patterns as the wave itself. It's good there are still spots like this next to uninhabited islands that are perfect, clean and empty.

CARIBBEAN
PHOTO: CHRIS BURKARD

Pat Gudauskas pulling into a barrel deep in the Caribbean. This ultra rare wave only worked for a couple of days and we got lucky enough to be there when it happened.

TEAHUPO'O, TAHITI
PHOTO: BEN THOUARD

This is Landon McNamara at Teahupo'o and definitely one of my favourite photos ever. Conditions were unreal that day.

TASMANIA
PHOTO: ANDREW CHISHOLM

A wise man once told me, "taking photos is all about the light", which is the case on this perfect wave rolling through on Tasmania's east coast. Shooting into the sun can at times be technically difficult, but often the results are epic!

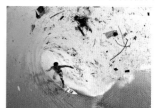

INDONESIA
PHOTO: ZAK NOYLE/A-FRAME

Dede Suryana and a shocking shot from remote Indonesia. Plastic pollution is a huge issue and this image went around the world raising awareness of the massive problem we all need to deal with.

EDDYSTONE ROCK
PHOTO: ANDREW CHISHOLM

This is what it's all about – clean, massive barrels with just your friends out. Located about 26km offshore south of Tasmania, this big wave slab has massive amounts of power. The injury to wave ridden ratio would have to be up there with the highest in the world. The area is brimming with marine life; Australasian gannets, black-faced cormorants and fairy prions are often seen there as well as Australian and New Zealand fur seals.

THE PIRATE ISLES, MADAGASCAR
PHOTO: ALAN VAN GYSEN

One of the last great unexplored stretches of coastline, Madagascar's east coast is littered with empty waves like these, thanks to the county's lack of accessibility and its far flung remoteness.

PIPELINE, HAWAII
PHOTO: JOSH TABONE

85mm is my preferred zoom length out at the infamous Banzai Pipeline. It's lightweight, very reliable and you can swim between the photog packs and still find cool perspectives. Here you see that I'm a little closer to the peak. Definitely one of my favourite waves to shoot in the world for sure.

TEAHUPO'O, TAHITI
PHOTO: BEN THOUARD

This is Koa Rothman at Teahupo'o in May 2013 during a big tow in swell we had. Laird Hamilton towed him into this wave, which ended up being the biggest wave of the swell.

ICELAND

PHOTO: CHRIS BURKARD

The Westfjords of Iceland, even to Icelandic standards, is somewhat of an unknown. With the promise of a massive swell approaching, we began our search and ended up finding some incredible waves such as this one.

INSTAGRAM_

ALAN VAN GYSEN @ALANVANGYSEN

ANDREW CHISHOLM @ANDYCHIZA

ANDREW SHIELD @ANDREWSHIELD

BASTIEN BONNARME @BASTIENBONNARME

BEN THOUARD @BENTHOUARD

CHRIS BURKARD @CHRISBURKARD

DAMIAN DAVILA @DAMIANDAVILAPHOTOS

HELIO ANTONIO @HELIO_ANTONIO

JOSH TABONE @JOSHUATABONE

LAURENT PUJOL @LAURENTPUJOL

MARCUS PALADINO @MARCUSPALADINO

MIKE LACEY @MIKELACEYPHOTO

RODD OWEN @OWENPHOTO

RYAN MILLER @BADBOYRYRY_

TIMO JARVINEN @GOTFILM

TRENT SLATTER @TRENTSLATTERPHOTO

ZAK NOYLE @ZAKNOYLE

THE ULTIMATE BEDROOM VIEW OF THURSO EAST. PHOTO: ROGER SHARP

Other titles from Orca Publications:

INCREDIBLE WAVES
by Chris Power
ISBN 978-0-9567893-3-4
£24.99

**SURF TRAVEL –
THE COMPLETE GUIDE**
by Sam Bleakley
ISBN 978-0-9567893-4-1
£17.99

**THE SURFING TRIBE:
A HISTORY OF SURFING
IN BRITAIN**
by Roger Mansfield
ISBN 978-0-9523646-0-3
£22.99

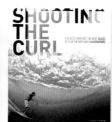

SHOOTING THE CURL
by Chris Power
ISBN 978-0-9523646-8-9
£22.99

**THE SURF GIRL HANDBOOK
SECOND EDITION**
by Louise Searle
ISBN 978-0-9567893-8-9
£17.99

**THE SURF GIRL GUIDE
TO SURF FITNESS**
by Louise Searle
ISBN 978-0-9567893-7-2
£17.99

**ADVANCED SURF FITNESS FOR
HIGH PERFORMANCE SURFING**
by Lee Stanbury
ISBN 978-0-9567893-9-6
£19.99

**THE COMPLETE GUIDE
TO SURF FITNESS**
by Lee Stanbury
ISBN 978-0-9523646-6-5
£19.99